LAW LIBRARY OF CONGRESS

August 28, 2006

A Series of Studies on

Presidential Power In Foreign Relations:
No. 1: The "Sole Organ" Doctrine

Louis Fisher[1]
Specialist in Constitutional Law

Executive Summary

The Executive Branch relies in part on the "sole organ" doctrine to define presidential power broadly in foreign relations and national security, including assertions of an inherent executive power that is not subject to legislative or judicial constraints. The doctrine draws from a statement by John Marshall when he served in the House of Representatives in 1800: "The President is the sole organ of the nation in its external relations, and its sole representative with foreign nations."[2] The Supreme Court, in United States *v.* Curtiss-Wright *(1936), cited Marshall's speech in arguing for inherent presidential powers in external relations. When read in context, however, Marshall's speech does not support an independent, extra-constitutional or exclusive power of the President in foreign relations. The concept of an Executive having sole power over foreign relations borrows from other sources, including the British model of a royal prerogative.*

I. Executive Branch Position

In offering a legal defense for President Harry Truman's decision in 1950 to order U.S. troops to Korea, the State Department argued that the President "has authority to conduct the foreign relations of the United States."[3] Citing *United States* v. *Curtiss-Wright* (1936), the department stated that the President is "charged with the duty of conducting the foreign relations of the United States and in this field he 'alone has the power to speak or listen as a representative of the Nation.'"[4] In 1966, the State Department defended the legality of the Vietnam War in part by stating that the President "holds the prime responsibility for the conduct of United States foreign relations."[5]

A more recent claim of exclusive or overriding presidential power appears in a 1996 memo by the Office of Legal Counsel (OLC) regarding a whistleblower bill for the Intelligence Community. OLC

---

[1] The author appreciates comments and suggestions from David Abramowitz, Reb Brownell, Mary Cornaby, Jennifer Elsea, Brian McKeon, Harold Relyea, Morton Rosenberg, Kersi Shroff, and Hillel Weinberg.

[2] 10 ANNALS OF CONG. 613.

[3] U.S. Department of State, *Authority of the President to Repel the Attack in Korea*, 23 Department of State Bulletin 173 (1950).

[4] *Id.* at 174.

[5] U.S. Department of State, *The Legality of United States Participation in the Defense of Viet-Nam*, 54 Department of State Bulletin 474, 484 (1966).

concluded that the bill was unconstitutional in part because of the President's role as "sole organ of the Nation in its external relations."[6] In a series of confidential memos written after 9/11, later released to the public, OLC wrote: "We conclude that the Constitution vests the President with the plenary authority, as Commander in Chief and the sole organ of the Nation in its foreign relations, to use military force abroad – especially in response to grave national emergencies created by sudden, unforeseen attacks on the people and territory of the United States." [7]

On January 19, 2006, OLC defended the authority of the National Security Agency (NSA) to intercept international communications coming into and going out of the United States of persons allegedly linked to al Qaeda or related terrorist organizations. In defending the legality of the NSA operation, OLC pointed to "the President's well-recognized inherent constitutional authority as Commander in Chief and sole organ for the Nation in foreign affairs . . . ."[8] In cases challenging NSA eavesdropping, the government argues in court that the state secrets privilege "embodies central aspects of the Executive's responsibilities under Article II of the Constitution as Commander-in-Chief and as the Nation's organ for foreign affairs."[9]

Referred to in this manner, the "sole organ" doctrine appears to support a plenary, exclusive and inherent authority of the President in foreign relations and national security, an authority that overrides conflicting statutes and treaties. The theory appears to carry special weight because its author is John Marshall, a member of the House in 1800 and later Chief Justice of the Supreme Court. The theory is developed in an important foreign affairs case, *United States* v. *Curtiss-Wright*.[10] However, when Marshall's speech is read in context, he did not advocate an independent, inherent presidential power over external affairs. That scope of power did exist in foreign constitutions and precedents, such as in British law, but Sections II through IV explain how the framers of the U.S. Constitution rejected the model of an Executive empowered to exercise exclusive control over external relations.[11]

II. British Precedents

In creating a republic, the framers of the U.S. Constitution broke with the monarchical and prerogative principles promoted by such writers as John Locke and William Blackstone. Locke and Blackstone wrote against the backdrop of the seventeenth-century struggle for power between the British Parliament and the King. Parliamentarians urged that law derived from popular control and legislative action; supporters of monarchy believed in centralized authority and the doctrine of divine immanence.[12]

---

[6] U.S. Department of Justice, Office of Legal Counsel, *Access to Classified Information*, by Christopher H. Schroeder, Acting Assistant Attorney General, Nov. 26, 1996, at 4 (citing a Justice Department brief).

[7] U.S. Department of Justice, Office of Legal Counsel, *The President's Constitutional Authority to Conduct Military Operations Against Terrorists and Nations Supporting Them*, by John C. Yoo, Deputy Assistant Attorney General, Sept. 25, 2001, at 1.

[8] U.S. Department of Justice, Office of Legal Counsel, Legal Authorities Supporting the Activities of the National Security Agency Described by the President, Jan. 19, 2006, at 1.

[9] United States' Reply in Support of the Assertion of the Military and State Secrets Privilege and Motion to Dismiss or, in the Alternative, for Summary Judgment by the United States, Hepting v. AT&T, Case No. C-06-0672-VRW (D. Cal. June 16, 2006), at 4.

[10] 299 U.S. 304, 319 (1936).

[11] By the 1600s, the British Parliament had begun to exercise some foreign affairs powers through the withholding and conditioning of funds, investigations, and impeachment of Cabinet officials. Abraham Sofaer, War, Foreign Affairs and Constitutional Power: The Origins 6-15 (1976).

[12] FRANCIS D. WORMUTH, THE ROYAL PREROGATIVE, 1603-1649, at 3-8 (1939).

To the royalists, the King exercised "not a derivative but a natural authority."[13] Those who wrote in defense of the royal prerogative argued that it "inheres in the scepter, [and] cannot be taken away by any act of Parliament."[14] By invoking the doctrine "reason of state," monarchs asserted their right to place individuals in jail "without naming a cause and to hold the prisoner without bail."[15]

In his *Second Treatise on Civil Government* (1690), Locke promoted a number of republican principles to counter monarchical powers. He spoke of separating government into three branches: legislative, executive, and "federative." The last power, however, is what is called today foreign policy, and consisted of "the power of war and peace, leagues and alliances, and all the transactions with all persons and communities without the commonwealth." The federative power, Locke said, was "always almost united" with the Executive. Any attempt to separate executive and federative powers, he warned, would invite "disorder and ruin."[16]

In his *Commentaries on the Law of England*, Blackstone placed all of foreign affairs and the war power in the Executive, who had the sole power to make war, send and receive ambassadors, make treaties, issue letters of marque and reprisals (authorizing private citizens to undertake military actions), and raise and regulate fleets and armies.[17] Those powers were exclusive and not subject to checks: "in the exertion of lawful prerogative, the king is, and ought to be absolute; that is, so far absolute, that there is no legal authority than can either delay or resist him."[18] The power over external affairs was "wisely placed in a single hand by the British constitution, for the sake of unanimity, strength, and dispatch."[19] In describing this exclusivity, Blackstone often resorted to the adjective "sole." Thus, the king "has the sole power of sending ambassadors to foreign states, and receiving ambassadors at home."[20] The king has "the sole prerogative of making war and peace."[21] The king has "the sole power of raising and regulating fleets and armies."[22] However broad the operation of the royal prerogative, it had limits. The Parliament could control the funding of fleets and armies. Moreover, the king's prerogative applied to "all things, that are not injurious to the subject [citizen]; for in them all, it must be remembered, that the king's prerogative stretcheth not to the doing of any wrong."[23]

The framers did not assign Blackstone's prerogatives over foreign affairs solely to the President. Some of those powers are given exclusively to Congress (such as the power to declare war, issue letters of marque and reprisal, and raise and support armies and navies). Others are shared between the Senate and the President (the power to appoint ambassadors and make treaties).[24] Under Article II, the President

---

[13] *Id.* at 9.

[14] *Id.* at 73.

[15] *Id.* at 78. See also H. V. EVATT, THE ROYAL PREROGATIVE (1987); JOHN ALLEN, INQUIRY INTO THE RISE AND GROWTH OF THE ROYAL PREROGATIVE IN ENGLAND (1849).

[16] JOHN LOCKE, SECOND TREATISE ON CIVIL GOVERNMENT §§ 146-48 (1690).

[17] 2 BLACKSTONE, COMMENTARIES ON THE LAWS OF ENGLAND 237-62 (1803). *See* HALSBURY'S LAWS OF ENGLAND, V.. 8(2), at 465, para. 801 (4th ed. 1996).

[18] 2 BLACKSTONE, COMMENTARIES, at 250.

[19] *Id.*

[20] *Id.* at 252.

[21] *Id.* at 257.

[22] *Id.* at 262.

[23] *Id.* at 238 (citing Finch L. 84, 85).

[24] U.S. CONST. arts. I-II.

"shall receive Ambassadors and other public Ministers," and he is the "Commander in Chief of the Army and Navy of the United States, and of the Militia of the several States, when called into the actual Service of the United States." As indicated by the nature of powers expressly granted to Congress in Article I, the Commander in Chief Clause could not have been meant to incorporate the powers of the British king.

Joseph Chitty, in his 1820 work on the prerogatives of the Crown, reflects the values and principles found in Blackstone. Chitty regarded it essential that the British constitution "made the King the delegate or representative of the people, with regard to foreign affairs; and has invested his Majesty with the supreme exclusive power of managing them."[25] To Chitty, the constitution vested in the king "the sole power" to send ambassadors, consuls, and other minister abroad.[26] As to letters of marque and reprisal, the king was "the only constitutional judge of the policy and expediency of commencing hostilities."[27] The king possessed "the exclusive right to make war or peace, either within or out of his dominions."[28]

III. Montesquieu's Influence

The framers of the U.S. Constitution paid great respect to Montesquieu, praising him in the *Federalist Papers* as "the celebrated Montesquieu" and the "oracle" always cited on the separation doctrine.[29] They accepted his argument that in order to form a moderate government "it is necessary to combine the several powers; to regulate, temper, and set them in motion; to give, as it were, ballast to one, in order to enable it to counterpoise the other."[30] They agreed also with these sentiments: "constant experience shows us that every man invested with power is apt to abuse it, and to carry his authority as far as it will go. Is it not strange, though true, to say that virtue itself has need of limits? To prevent this abuse, it is necessary from the very nature of things that power should be a check to power."[31]

With regard to foreign relations, however, Montesquieu appeared to associate this field of action solely with the executive power. He recognized that the prince or magistrate "makes peace or war, sends or receives embassies, establishes the public security, and provides against invasions."[32] He divided the executive power into two parts, one with respect "to things dependent on the law of nations," and the other with regard "to matters that depend on the civil law."[33] By linking the Executive to the law of nations, the power of war came with it: "Offensive force is regulated by the law of nations."[34] Governments — meaning the executive power — "have a right to wage war for their own preservation."[35]

---

[25] JOSEPH CHITTY, A TREATISE ON THE LAW OF THE PREROGATIVES OF THE CROWN 40 (1820).

[26] *Id.*

[27] *Id.* at 40-41.

[28] *Id.* at 41. *See also* A. W. BRADLEY ET AL., CONSTITUTIONAL AND ADMINISTRATIVE LAW 324-25 (11th ed. 1996).

[29] THE FEDERALIST NO. 47 (James Madison); THE FEDERALIST 353 (Cooke ed. 1961).

[30] BARON DE MONTESQUIEU, THE SPIRIT OF LAWS 62 (1949).

[31] *Id.* at 150.

[32] *Id.* at 151.

[33] *Id.*

[34] *Id.* at 133.

[35] *Id.*

IV. Republican Form of Government

The framers rejected Blackstone's and Montesquieu's theory of foreign relations because they put their trust not in a single Executive to govern foreign relations but in a system of popular control, elected representatives, separation of powers, and checks and balances. In Federalist No. 39, James Madison spoke about a government "which derives all its powers directly or indirectly from the great body of the people."[36] This choice of government necessarily placed the primary power and authority in Congress. Madison underscored the vital link between a republican form of government and the spirit that infused the American Revolution: "[N]o other form would be reconcilable with the genius of the people of America; with the fundamental principles of the revolution; or with that honorable determination, which animates every votary of freedom, to rest all our political experiments on the capacity of mankind for self-government. If the plan of the Convention therefore be found to depart from the republican character, its advocates must abandon it as no longer defensible."[37] Elsewhere in *The Federalist*, Madison emphasized that "[i]n republican government the legislative authority, necessarily, predominates."[38]

Alexander Hamilton, generally supportive of executive authority, offered these words of caution in Federalist No. 75 about the process of treaty-making: "The history of human conduct does not warrant that exalted opinion of human virtue which would make it wise in a nation to commit interests of so delicate and momentous a kind as those which concern its intercourse with the rest of the world to the sole disposal of a magistrate, created and circumstanced, as would be a president of the United States."[39]

When the delegates met at the Philadelphia Convention in 1787, the British war model of Blackstone was repeatedly criticized. Pierce Butler "was for vesting the power in the President, who will have all the requisite qualities, and will not make war but when the Nation will support it." Roger Sherman, however, argued that the President should "be able to repel and not to commence war." Responding to Butler's statement, Elbridge Gerry objected that he "never expected to hear in a republic a motion to empower the Executive alone to declare war."[40] George Mason "was agst giving the power of war to the Executive, because not <safely> to be trusted with it; . . . He was for clogging rather than facilitating war; but for facilitating peace."[41]

During the constitutional debates, Charles Pinckney said he was for "a vigorous Executive but was afraid the Executive powers of <the existing> Congress might extend to peace & war &c which would render the Executive a Monarchy, of the worse kind, towit an elective one."[42] John Rutledge wanted the executive power placed in a single person, "tho' he was not for giving him the power of war and peace."[43] James Wilson, also supporting a single executive, "did not consider the Prerogatives of the British Monarch as a proper guide in defining the Executive powers. Some of these prerogatives were of a Legislative nature. Among others that of war & peace &c."[44] Edmund Randolph worried about

---

[36] THE FEDERALIST 252 (Jacob E. Cooke ed. 1961).

[37] *Id.* at 250.

[38] *Id.* at 350 (FEDERALIST NO. 51).

[39] *Id.* at 548 (FEDERALIST NO. 75).

[40] 2 THE RECORDS OF THE FEDERAL CONVENTION OF 1787, at 318 (M. Farrand ed., 1937) (hereafter "Farrand").

[41] *Id.* at 319.

[42] 1 Farrand 64-65.

[43] *Id.* at 65.

[44] *Id.* at 65-66.

executive power, calling it "the fœtus of monarchy."[45] The delegates at the Philadelphia convention, he said, had "no motive to be governed by the British Governmt. as our prototype."[46] If the United States had no other choice he might adopt the British model, but "the fixt genius of the people of America required a different form of Government."[47] Wilson agreed that the British model "was inapplicable to the situation of this Country; the extent of which was so great, and the manners so republican, that nothing but a great confederated Republic would do for it."[48]

The framers underscored their concerns about presidential wars. In *The Federalist No. 4*, John Jay warned that "nations in general will make war whenever they have a prospect of getting any thing by it, nay that absolute monarchs will often make war when their nations are to get nothing by it, but for purposes and objects merely personal, such as, a thirst for military glory, revenge for personal affronts; ambition, or private compacts to aggrandize or support their particular families, or partizans. These and a variety of motives, which affect only the mind of the Sovereign, often lead him to engage in wars not sanctified by justice, or the voice and interests of his people."[49]

In 1793, Madison called war "the true nurse of executive aggrandizement. . . . In war, the honours and emoluments of office are to be multiplied; and it is the executive patronage under which they are to be enjoyed. It is in war, finally, that laurels are to be gathered; and it is the executive brow they are to encircle. The strongest passions and most dangerous weaknesses of the human breast; ambition, avarice, vanity, the honourable or venial love of fame, are all in conspiracy against the desire and duty of peace."[50] Five years later, in a letter to Thomas Jefferson, Madison emphasized that the Constitution "supposes, what the History of all Govts demonstrates, that the Ex. is the branch of power most interested in war, & most prone to it. It has accordingly with studied care, vested the question of war in the Legisl."[51]

Joseph Story, who served on the Supreme Court as Associate Justice from 1811 to 1845, offered similar observations. The power of declaring war "is in its own nature and effects so critical and calamitous, that it requires the utmost deliberation, and the successive review of all the councils of the nation," for it "never fails to impose upon the people the most burthensome taxes, and personal sufferings."[52] War "is sometimes fatal to public liberty itself, by introducing a spirit of military glory, which is ready to follow, wherever a successful commander will lead; and in a republic, whose institutions are essentially founded on the basis of peace, there is infinite danger, that war will find it both imbecile in defense and eager for contest."[53] Further: "the history of republics has but too fatally proved, that they are too ambitious of military fame and conquest, and too easily devoted to the views of

---

[45] *Id.* at 66.

[46] *Id.*

[47] *Id.*

[48] *Id.*

[49] THE FEDERALIST 26 (Jacob E. Cooke ed., 1961).

[50] 6 THE WRITINGS OF JAMES MADISON 174 (Gaillard Hunt ed., 1906).

[51] *Id.* at 312.

[52] 3 JOSEPH STORY, COMMENTARIES ON THE CONSTITUTION OF THE UNITED STATES 60 (1833, reprinted by Rothman & Co., 1991).

[53] *Id.* at 61.

demagogues, who flatter their pride, and betray their interests. It should therefore be difficult in a republic to declare war; but not to make peace."[54]

V. Marshall's Speech

Against this backdrop, one can better understand the scope and purpose of the speech by Rep. John Marshall. During debate on March 7, 1800, in the House of Representatives, he called the President "the sole organ of the nation in its external relations, and its sole representative with foreign nations."[55] The context of his speech demonstrates that his intent was not to advocate inherent or exclusive executive power, much less the powers of a British monarch. As shown below, Marshall's objective was to defend the authority of President John Adams to carry out an extradition treaty. The President was not the "sole organ" in formulating the treaty. He was the sole organ in *implementing* it. Article II of the Constitution specifies that it is the President's duty to "take Care that the Laws be faithfully executed," and in Article VI, all treaties made "shall be the supreme Law of the Land."

During the debate in 1800, opponents of President Adams insisted that he should be impeached or censured for turning over to England someone charged with murder. Because the case was already pending in an American court, some lawmakers urged that action be taken against him for encroaching upon the judiciary and violating the doctrine of separation of powers. Yet Adams had operated under the extradition article (Article 27) of the Jay Treaty, which provided that the United States and Great Britain would deliver up to each other "all persons" charged with murder or forgery.[56] The debate began with a member of the House requesting that President Adams provide documents "relative to, the apprehension and delivering of Jonathan Robbins, under the twenty-seventh article" of the treaty.[57] Although critics of the President claimed that Robbins was "a citizen of the United States,"[58] Secretary of State Timothy Pickering regarded Robbins as an assumed name for Thomas Nash, a native Irishman.[59] U.S. District Judge Thomas Bee, who was asked to turn the prisoner over to the British, considered the individual to be Thomas Nash.[60] A House resolution described President Adam's decision to turn the accused over to the British "a dangerous interference of the Executive with Judicial decisions."[61] Some members questioned whether the House had the power "to censure or to approbate the conduct of the Executive."[62] Others saw the debate heading in the direction of impeachment.[63]

---

[54] *Id.*

[55] 10 ANNALS OF CONG. 613 (1800), *cited in* United States v. Curtiss-Wright Corp., 299 U.S. 304, 319 (1936).

[56] "It is further agreed, that his Majesty and the United States, on mutual requisitions, by them respectively, or by their respective ministers or officers authorized to make the same, will deliver up to justice all persons, who, being charged with murder or forgery, committed within the jurisdiction of either, shall seek asylum within any of the countries of the other, provided that this shall only be done on such evidence of criminality, as, according to the laws of the place, where the fugitive or person so charged shall be found, would justify his apprehension and commitment for trial, if the offence had there been committed. The expence of such apprehension and delivery shall be borne and defrayed, by those who make the requisition and receive the fugitive." Art. 27 of the Treaty with Great Britain, Nov. 19, 1794, 8 Stat. 129.

[57] 10 ANNALS OF CONG. 511 (1800).

[58] *Id.* (statement by Rep. Livingston).

[59] *Id.* at 515.

[60] *Id.* See United States v. Robins [sic], 27 Fed. Cas. 825, 832 (1799) (Case No. 16,175). The proceedings before Judge Bee are also reprinted in FRANCIS WHARTON, STATE TRIALS OF THE UNITED STATES 392-457 (1849).

[61] 10 ANNALS OF CONG. 533.

[62] *Id.* at 551 (statement by Rep. Craik).

[63] *Id.* (statement by Rep. Harper).

Five months before the House debate began, John Marshall had written an article for the *Virginia Federalist* (Richmond) on September 7, 1799, setting forth his analysis of the dispute over what he called "the case of Robbins."[64] He explained that on matters of extradition, nations communicate with each other "through the channel of their governments," and the "natural, and obvious and the proper mode is an application on the part of the government (requiring the fugitive) to the executive of the nation to which he has fled, to secure and cause him to be delivered up."[65] The concept of "sole organ," then, included this capacity of the President to act as the channel for communication with other nations. In carrying out Article 27 of the Jay Treaty, Marshall said that President Adams "[u]pon the whole . . . appears to have done no more than his duty."[66] By implementing this provision of the treaty, President Adams had "execute[d] one of the supreme laws of the land, which he was bound to observe and have carried into effect."[67] Nothing in this analysis suggested an inherent or exclusive role for the President. Once the President and the Senate had agreed on a treaty, it was the President's duty to see that the treaty was faithfully executed, as with any other law.

Having honed his major arguments, Marshall was prepared to respond to the House resolutions of possible censure or even impeachment. After listening to the debate in 1800, he took the floor to say that there were no grounds to rebuke the President. In matters such as carrying out an extradition provision in a treaty, "a case like that of Thomas Nash is a case for Executive and not Judicial decision."[68] Here is the "sole organ" comment in full:

> The President is the sole organ of the nation in its external relations, and its sole representative with foreign nations. Of consequence, the demand of a foreign nation can only be made on him.
> He possesses the whole Executive power. He holds and directs the force of the nation. Of consequence, any act to be performed by the force of the nation is to be performed through him.
> He is charged to execute the laws. A treaty is declared to be a law. He must then execute a treaty, where he, and he alone, possesses the means of executing it.
> The treaty, which is a law, enjoins the performance of a particular object. The person who is to perform this object is marked out by the Constitution, since the person is named who conducts the foreign intercourse, and is to take care that the laws be faithfully executed. The means by which it is to be performed, the force of the nation, are in the hands of this person. Ought not this person to perform the object, although the particular mode of using the means has not been prescribed? Congress, unquestionably, may prescribe the mode, and Congress may devolve on others the whole execution of the contract; but, till this be done, it seems the duty of the Executive department to execute the contract by any means it possesses.[69]

Marshall emphasized that President Adams had not attempted to make foreign policy single-handedly. He was carrying out a policy made jointly by the President and the Senate (for treaties). Only after the policy had been formulated through the collective effort of the executive and legislative branches, either by treaty or by statute, did the President emerge as the "sole organ" in implementing national policy. It was the President's constitutional duty to carry out the law, including treaties, however

---

[64] 4 THE PAPERS OF JOHN MARSHALL 23 (Cullen ed., 1984).

[65] *Id.* at 25.

[66] *Id.* at 28.

[67] *Id.*

[68] 10 ANNALS OF CONG. 611 (1800).

[69] *Id.* at 613-14.

"Congress, unquestionably, may prescribe the mode."[70] Marshall also recognized that there were limits on the President's authority to make law where Congress had not provided it: "And although the Executive cannot supply a total Legislative omission, yet it is not admitted or believed that there is such a total omission in this case."[71]

What if Thomas Nash had been an American and pressed into service on the British ship *Hermione*, where he committed murder? Could he have been transferred to England and tried and executed there? Marshall denied that could be so: "Had Thomas Nash been an impressed American, the homicide on board the Hermione would, most certainly, not have been a murder. The act of impressing an American is an act of lawless violence. The confinement on board a vessel is a continuation of the violence, and an additional outrage."[72]

Some scholars have interpreted Marshall's "sole organ" remark as the President merely being the organ of communication with another nation. Leonard W. Levy wrote that the President as sole organ "meant nothing more than that only the president communicates with foreign nations; he is the organ of communication."[73] To Harold Koh, Marshall's remarks about the President as sole organ "were uncontroversial, not because Congress had accepted a broad presidential monopoly over all foreign relations, but because it had largely acquiesced in the president's narrower dominance over diplomatic communications."[74] Marshall's remarks during the debate of 1800 demonstrate that he meant both communications with other nations and the President's duty to carry treaties into effect.

Edward S. Corwin, in his classic work *The President*, said that what Marshall had "foremost in mind" in describing the President as sole organ "was simply the President's role as *instrument of communication* with other governments."[75] He concluded: "*there is no more securely established principle of constitutional practice than the exclusive right of the President to be the nation's intermediary in its dealing with other nations.*"[76] This emphasis on communication of national policy with other countries did not include a form of inherent power incapable of being checked by other branches of government.

VI. Influences on Marshall

Marshall's formulation of the sole-organ theory built on earlier observations about the authority of a Chief Executive to communicate national policy to other countries. When John Locke spoke of the "federative power" (the exercise of authority over foreign affairs), he included within those executive duties "all the transactions with all persons and communities without the commonwealth." Thomas

---

[70] For example, a statute in 1848 provided that in all cases of treaties of extradition between the United States and another country, federal and state judges were authorized to determine whether the evidence was sufficient to sustain the charge against the individual to be extradited. 9 Stat. 320 (1848); *In re* Kaine, 55 U.S. 103, 111-14 (1852).

[71] *Id.* at 614.

[72] *Id.* at 617. For efforts by the Jeffersonians to use the Robbins affair for political advantage during the election of 1800, see Ruth Wedgwood, *The Revolutionary Martydom of Jonathan Robbins*, 100 YALE L. J. 229, 311-61 (1990); Larry C. Cress, *The Jonathan Robbins Incident: Extradition and the Separation of Powers in the Adams Administration*, 111 Essex Institute Historical Collection 99, 106-16 (1975); and DONALD H. STEWART, THE OPPOSITION PRESS OF THE FEDERALIST PERIOD 242-47 (1969).

[73] LEONARD W. LEVY, ORIGINAL INTENT AND THE FRAMERS' CONSTITUTION 52 (1988).

[74] HAROLD HONGJU KOH, THE NATIONAL SECURITY CONSTITUTION 81 (1990).

[75] EDWARD S. CORWIN, THE PRESIDENT 178 (4th ed. 1957) (emphasis in original).

[76] *Id.* at 184 (emphasis in original).

Jefferson, serving as Secretary of State in 1790, also used the word "transactions" regarding foreign policy. He wrote: "The transaction of business with foreign nations is Executive altogether. It belongs then to the head of that department, *except* as to such portions of it as are specially submitted to the Senate. *Exceptions* are to be construed strictly."[77]

This passage from Jefferson is sometimes read to define presidential power broadly and exclusively in foreign affairs. By making the transaction of business with foreign nations "Executive altogether," it has been argued that the Constitution makes foreign policy "an executive prerogative."[78] However, Jefferson wrote about a very narrow dispute concerning the Senate's role in the appointment of ambassadors and consuls. President George Washington had asked Jefferson whether the Senate had a right to veto the appointee and decide what *grade* the President might want for a foreign mission.[79] Jefferson concluded that if the Constitution intended to give the Senate power to veto the grade, "it would have said so in direct terms, and not left it to be effected by a sidewind."[80] In responding to this specific issue, Jefferson had no reason to address the larger role of Congress in foreign affairs or the particular prerogatives of the House, such as the power to grant or withhold legislation and appropriations.

Jefferson spoke of *transactions*, which means some kind of communication between two parties. In that sense, Jefferson's statement is consistent with Marshall's in 1800. Whenever Congress and the President act jointly to formulate foreign policy, it is the President who communicates, transmits, and explains that policy to other nations. Presidents may initiate foreign policies of their own, such as the Monroe Policy, but those executive statements of national policy survive only with congressional acquiescence. Through authorizations, appropriations, and other powers, Congress can revoke or modify presidential initiatives in foreign policy.

During the controversy over President Washington's issuance of the Neutrality Proclamation in 1793, competing definitions of presidential power were offered. In one of his "Pacificus" essays, Alexander Hamilton wrote that the "legislative department is not the *organ* of intercourse between the United States and foreign nations."[81] The executive department is "the *organ* of intercourse between the nation and foreign nations."[82] Through this language, Hamilton did not adopt the Blackstonian view of exclusive executive power over foreign affairs. He understood that under the U.S. Constitution "the Legislature can alone declare war, can alone actually transfer the nation from a state of peace to a state of hostility . . . ."[83] Writing a few months later, Jefferson made the same observation about the "right to go to war." The U.S. Constitution, he agreed, "gives that power to Congress alone."[84]

On November 22, 1793, Jefferson wrote to the French Minister, Edmond Charles Genet, that the President was "the only channel of communication between this country and foreign nations, [and] it is from him alone that foreign nations or their agents are to learn what is or has been the will of the

---

[77] 16 THE PAPERS OF THOMAS JEFFERSON 379 (Boyd ed. 1961) (emphasis in original).

[78] H. JEFFERSON POWELL, THE PRESIDENT'S AUTHORITY OVER FOREIGN AFFAIRS 45-46 (2002). *See also* JOHN YOO, THE POWERS OF WAR AND PEACE 19 (2005).

[79] 16 THE PAPERS OF THOMAS JEFFERSON 379 (Boyd ed.)

[80] Id. at 380.

[81] PACIFICUS NO. 1, June 29, 1793; 4 THE WORKS OF ALEXANDER HAMILTON 436 (Lodge ed. 1904) (emphasis in original).

[82] *Id.* at 437 (emphasis in original).

[83] *Id.* at 443.

[84] Letter to Gouverneur Morris, Aug. 16, 1793; 6 THE WRITINGS OF THOMAS JEFFERSON 381 (Ford ed. 1895).

nation."[85]   This appears to be consistent with Marshall's sole-organ speech in 1800. The will of the nation represented a reflection of presidential-congressional actions through the legislative and treaty processes, after which the President became the channel for communicating that will.

Writing on May 12, 1798, Hamilton again expressed his understanding of the degree to which the U.S. Constitution broke with the Blackstonian model. American ships at sea were always entitled to repel force by force and to repress hostilities within U.S. waters, but "Any thing beyond this must fall under the idea of reprisals & requires the sanction of that Department which is to declare or make war."[86] Jefferson had earlier, in 1793, reached the same conclusion: "if the case were important enough to require reprisal, & ripe for that step, Congress must be called on to take it; the right of reprisal being expressly lodged with them by the constitution, & not with the executive."[87]

VII. Marshall on the Court

In his capacity as Chief Justice of the Supreme Court, Marshall held to his position that the making of foreign policy is a joint exercise by the executive and legislative branches (through treaties and statutes), not a unilateral or exclusive authority of the President. Blackstone's theory of external relations, the British royal prerogative, and the concept of inherent executive power in foreign affairs do not appear in Marshall's decisions. With the war power, for example, Marshall looked solely to Congress — not the President — for the authority to take the country to war against another power.

He wrote for the Court in *Talbot* v. *Seeman* (1801), a case involving salvage of the ship *Amelia* as a result of the Quasi-War with France. Part of the decision turned on the undeclared nature of the war. A series of statutes had authorized President John Adams to use military force against France, but there had been no formal declaration of war. The Court the previous year had decided that Congress could authorize hostilities either way: by formal declaration or by statutory authority.[88]

In *Talbot*, the captain of a U.S. ship of war captured a merchant ship that the French had earlier seized. The owner of the ship sued the captain. Treating the seizure as legal, Chief Justice Marshall ruled in favor of the captain. To decide the case, it was necessary to examine the relationship between the United States and France at the time and Marshall looked for guidance exclusively to statutory policy: "To determine the real situation in regard to France, the acts of congress are to be inspected."[89] Marshall had no difficulty in identifying the branch that possessed the war power: "The whole powers of war being, by the constitution of the United States, vested in congress, the acts of that body can alone be resorted to as our guides in this enquiry."[90]

In an 1804 case, Chief Justice Marshall ruled that when a presidential proclamation issued in time of war was contrary to a statute enacted by Congress, the statute prevailed. As part of legislation involving the Quasi-War against France, Congress authorized the President to instruct naval commanders to stop and examine suspected U.S. ships "sailing *to* any port or place within the territory of the French Republic."[91] President John Adams, however, ordered naval commanders to stop and examine ships

---

[85] 6 THE WRITINGS OF THOMAS JEFFERSON 451 (Ford. ed. 1895).

[86] 21 THE PAPERS OF ALEXANDER HAMILTON 462 (Syrett ed. 1974).

[87] 6 The Writings of Thomas Jefferson 259 (Ford ed.).

[88] Bas v. Tingy, 4 U.S. 37 (1800).

[89] Talbot v. Seeman, 5 U.S. 1, 29 (1801).

[90] *Id.* at 28.

[91] 1 Stat. 615, § 5 (1799) (emphasis added).

sailing *"to, or from"* French ports.[92] Marshall conceded that "the first bias of my mind was very strong" in supporting the presidential proclamation and the actions of the naval commander who complied with it.

> That implicit obedience which military men usually pay to the orders of their superiors, which indeed is indispensably necessary to every military system, appeared to me strongly to imply the principle that those orders, if not to perform a prohibited act, ought to justify the person whose general duty it is to obey them, and who is placed by the laws of his country in a situation which in general requires that he should obey them.[93]

As he thought through the issue, Marshall became convinced "that I was mistaken, and I receded from this first opinion." He agreed with other Justices that presidential "instructions cannot change the nature of the transaction, or legalize an act which without those instructions would have been a plain trespass."[94] Having followed a presidential proclamation contrary to an act of Congress, Captain George Little "must be answerable in damages to the owner of this neutral vessel."[95] Congress later considered and passed a private bill to reimburse Captain Little for the damages awarded against him.[96]

In his celebrated opinion in *Marbury* v. *Madison* (1803), Chief Justice Marshall recognized a field of presidential actions that was political, exclusive in nature, and not subject to checks from the judiciary. Those actions, however, did not create a privileged area for the President with regard to foreign affairs, external affairs, or national security. Here is his language:

> By the constitution of the United States, the president is invested with certain important political powers, in the exercise of which he is to use his own discretion, and is accountable only to his country in his political character and to his own conscience. To aid him in the performance of these duties, he is authorized to appoint certain officers, who act by his authority, and in conformity with his orders.
>
> In such cases, their acts are his acts; and whatever opinion may be entertained of the matter in which executive discretion may be used, still there exists, and can exist, no power to control that discretion. The subjects are political. They respect the nation, not individual rights, and being intrusted to the executive, the decision of the executive is conclusive. The application of this remark will be perceived by adverting to the act of congress for establishing the department of foreign affairs. This officer, as his duties were prescribed by that act, is to conform precisely to the will of the president. He is the mere organ by whom that will is communicated. The acts of such an officer, as an officer, can never be examinable by the courts.
>
> But when the legislature proceeds to impose on that officer other duties; when he is directed peremptorily to perform certain acts; when the rights of individuals are dependent on the performance of those acts; he is so far the officer of the law; is amenable to the laws for his conduct; and cannot at his discretion sport away the vested rights of others.

---

[92] Little v. Barreme, 2 Cr. (6 U.S.) 170, 171 (1804).

[93] *Id.* at 179.

[94] *Id.*

[95] *Id.*

[96] 6 Stat. 63, ch. IV (1807); ANNALS OF CONG., 9th Cong., 2d Sess. 230-31 (1806), 29, 30, 31, 32, 253, 260-61 (1807). For House committee report, see American State Papers, Class 6, Naval Affairs, Vol. 1 (1834), at 138-39. The floor debate does not explain the reasons for congressional action, but lawmakers may have decided that federal law failed to adequately distinguish between lawful and unlawful orders. In 1789, Congress had directed military officers "to observe and obey the orders of the President of the United States." 1 Stat. 96, § 3 (1789). Legislation in 1799 provided that any officer "who shall disobey the orders of his superior . . . on any pretence whatsoever" shall be subject to death or other punishment. 1 Stat. 711 (1799) (Art. 24). Not until 1800, after Captain Little had seized the vessel, did Congress clarify the duty of military officers. They were not directed to carry out any and all commands. Instead, they faced punishment only when disobeying "the lawful orders of his superior officer." 2 Stat. 47 (1800) (Art. 14).

The conclusion from this reasoning is, that where the heads of departments are the political or confidential agents of the executive, merely to execute the will of the president, or rather to act in cases in which the executive possesses a constitutional or legal discretion, nothing can be more perfectly clear than that their acts are only politically examinable. But where a specific duty is assigned by law, and individual rights depend upon the performance of that duty, it seems equally clear that the individual who considers himself injured, has a right to resort to the laws of his country for a remedy.[97]

The President's "conclusive" and wholly discretionary decisions applied to orders given to executive officers appointed to carry out his policies. Actions by those officers "can never be examinable by the courts" *unless* Congress intervened to impose statutory duties on the officers. At that point courts are available to interpret those duties and the individual rights attached to them. Marshall said that if the head of an executive department "commits any illegal act, under colour of his office, by which an individual sustains an injury, it cannot be pretended that his office alone exempts him from being sued in the ordinary mode of proceeding, and being compelled to obey the judgment of the law."[98] That principle applied to both domestic and external affairs, as can be seen in the case of Captain Little.

VIII. The *Curtiss-Wright* Decision

Although the Court's decision in *Curtiss-Wright* is a standard citation for the "sole organ" doctrine and the existence of inherent executive power in the field of foreign affairs, the case itself did not concern independent presidential power. The issue before the judiciary was whether Congress had delegated *legislative* power too broadly when it authorized the President to declare an arms embargo in South America. A joint resolution by Congress allowed the President to prohibit the sale of arms in the Chaco region whenever he found that it "may contribute to the reestablishment of peace" between belligerents.[99]

In imposing the embargo, President Franklin D. Roosevelt relied solely on statutory — not inherent — authority. His proclamation prohibiting the sale of arms and munitions to countries engaged in armed conflict in the Chaco begins: "NOW, THEREFORE, I, FRANKLIN D. ROOSEVELT, President of the United States of America, acting under and by virtue of the authority conferred in me by the said joint resolution of Congress, ..."[100] The proclamation does not assert any inherent, independent, extra-constitutional, or exclusive presidential power.

It has been argued that the joint resolution passed by Congress was not really law but something inferior to it: "In the strictest sense, Congress did not choose to legislate in this case. It did not pass a statute that would act generally and prospectively; a statute that would bar arms to any nations engaged in an armed conflict."[101] Congress "acted, instead, through the device of a joint resolution."[102] The embargo imposed by President Roosevelt "seemed to be supported, in this case, by an act of Congress, but that act of Congress did not have the solemnity and the properties of a statute."[103] However, a joint

---

[97] Marbury v. Madison, 5 U.S. (1 Cr.) 137, 165-66 (1803).

[98] *Id.* at 170.

[99] 48 Stat. 811, ch. 365 (1934).

[100] *Id.* at 1745.

[101] HADLEY ARKES, THE RETURN OF GEORGE SUTHERLAND: RESTORING A JURISPRUDENCE OF NATURAL RIGHTS 198 (1994).

[102] *Id.*

[103] *Id.* at 204.

resolution has the identical legal properties of a bill that passes Congress and is enacted into law. Both must pass the two Houses. Both must be presented to the President and signed into law (or have both Houses override a veto). Joint resolutions are legally binding; simple and/or concurrent resolutions are not. Joint resolutions are often used in critically important legislation involving international relations and the use of military force. Roosevelt's proclamation indicated that he was acting solely under statutory, not some sort of "sense of Congress," non-binding resolution.

A. District Court and Briefs to the Supreme Court

Litigation on the proclamation focused on legislative power because, during the previous year, the Court, in two cases, had struck down the delegation by Congress of *domestic* power to the President.[104] The issue in *Curtiss-Wright* was whether Congress could delegate legislative power more broadly in international affairs than it could in domestic affairs. A district court, holding that the joint resolution represented an unconstitutional delegation of legislative authority, said nothing about any reservoir of inherent presidential power.[105] It acknowledged the "traditional practice of Congress in reposing the widest discretion in the Executive Department of the government in the conduct of the delicate and nicely posed issues of international relations."[106] Recognizing that need, however, did not save the delegation.

The district court decision was taken directly to the Supreme Court, where none of the briefs on either side discussed the availability of independent or inherent powers for the President. To the Justice Department, regarding the issue of jurisdiction, the question for the Court went to "the very power of Congress to delegate to the Executive authority to investigate and make findings in order to implement a legislative purpose."[107] The government's brief focused on whether the district court erred in holding that the joint resolution "constitutes an improper delegation of legislative power to the President."[108] The government argued that previous decisions by the Supreme Court, including those in the field of foreign relations, supported the delegation of this legislative power to the President.[109] Past delegations covering the domain of foreign relations represented "a valid exercise of legislative authority."[110] The joint resolution, said the government, contained adequate standards to guide the President and did not fall prey to the "unfettered discretion" found by the Court in the 1935 *Panama Refining* and *Schechter* decisions.[111]

The brief for the private company, Curtiss-Wright, also focused on the issue of delegated legislative power and did not explore the existence of independent or inherent presidential power. The brief charged that the joint resolution (1) represented an unlawful delegation of legislative power, (2) did

---

[104] Panama Refining Co. v. Ryan, 293 U.S. 388 (1935); Schechter Corp. v. United States, 295 U.S. 495 (1935).

[105] United States v. Curtiss-Wright Export Corp., 14 F. Supp. 230 (S.D.N.Y. 1936).

[106] *Id.* at 240.

[107] Statement as to Jurisdiction, United States v. Curtiss-Wright, No. 98, Supreme Court, October Term, 1936, signed by Martin Conboy, Special Assistant to the Attorney General of the United States, at 7; reprinted in 32 LANDMARK BRIEFS AND ARGUMENTS OF THE SUPREME COURT OF THE UNITED STATES: CONSTITUTIONAL LAW (Kurland and Casper eds., 1975), at 898 (hereafter "Landmark Briefs").

[108] Brief for the United States, Curtiss-Wright Export Corp., No. 98, Supreme Court, October Term, 1936, at 2; 32 Landmark Briefs 906.

[109] *Id.* at 6; 32 LANDMARK BRIEFS 910.

[110] *Id.* at 8; 32 LANDMARK BRIEFS 912.

[111] *Id.* at 16; 32 LANDMARK BRIEFS 920.

not go into operation because the President's proclamation failed to contain all the findings required by the joint resolution, (3) the President could not have consulted other governments as contemplated by the joint resolution, and (4) the effect of the President's second proclamation of November 14, 1935 extinguished the alleged liability of private companies involved in selling arms and munitions abroad.[112] A separate brief, prepared for other private parties, also concentrated on the delegation of legislative power.[113]

There was no need for the Supreme Court to explore the existence of independent, inherent, or exclusive presidential powers. Nevertheless, in extensive dicta, the decision by Justice Sutherland went far beyond the specific issue before the Court and discussed extra-constitutional powers of the President. Many of the themes in this decision were drawn from his writings as a U.S. Senator from Utah. According to his biographer, Sutherland "had long been the advocate of a vigorous diplomacy which strongly, even belligerently, called always for an assertion of American rights. It was therefore to be expected that [Woodrow] Wilson's cautious, sometimes pacifistic, approach excited in him only contempt and disgust."[114]

B. Senator Sutherland

Justice Sutherland had been a two-term Senator from Utah, serving from March 4, 1905 to March 3, 1917, and a member of the Senate Foreign Relations Committee. His opinion in *Curtiss-Wright* closely tracks his article, "The Internal and External Powers of the National Government," printed as a Senate document in 1910.[115] The article began with this fundamental principle: "That this Government is one of *limited* powers, and that absolute power resides nowhere except in the people, no one whose judgment is of any value has ever seriously denied . . . ."[116]

Yet subsequent analysis in the article moved in the direction of independent presidential power that could not be checked or limited by other branches, even by the people's representatives in Congress. He first faulted other studies for failing "to distinguish between our *internal* and our *external* relations."[117] As to the first category, he said the states possessed "every power not delegated to the General Government, or prohibited by the Constitution of the United States or the state constitution."[118] With regard to external relations, Sutherland argued that after the Declaration of Independence, the American colonies lost their character as free and independent states and that national sovereignty passed then to the central government.[119] In the article, Sutherland connects external matters with the national

---

[112] Brief for Appellees, Curtiss-Wright Export Corp. and Curtiss Aeroplane & Motor Co., Inc., United States v. Curtiss-Wright Export Corp., No. 98, Supreme Court, October Term, 1936, at 3; 32 LANDMARK BRIEFS 937.

[113] Brief for Appellees John S. Allard, Clarence W. Webster and Samuel J. Abelow, United States v. Curtiss-Wright Export Corp., No. 98, Supreme Court, October Term, 1936, at 3-5; 32 LANDMARK BRIEFS 979-81.

[114] JOEL FRANCIS PASCHAL, MR. JUSTICE SUTHERLAND: A MAN AGAINST THE STATE 93 (1951).

[115] S. Doc. No. 417, 61st Cong., 2d Sess. (1910).

[116] S. Doc. No. 417, at 1 (emphasis in original).

[117] *Id.* (emphasis in original).

[118] *Id.* at 3.

[119] "The Declaration of Independence asserted it when that great instrument declared that the *United* Colonies as free and independent States (that is, as *United* States, not as *separate* States) 'have full power to levy war, conclude peace, contract alliances, establish commerce, and *to do all other acts and things which independent States may of right do.*' And so national sovereignty inhered in the United States from the beginning. Neither the Colonies nor the States which succeeded them ever separately exercised authority over foreign affairs." *Id.* (emphasis in original).

government,[120] but in *Curtiss-Wright* he would associate national sovereignty and external affairs with the presidency, greatly expanding executive power. In addition to identifying express and implied constitutional powers in his article, Sutherland spoke of "inherent" powers and "extra-constitutional" powers.[121]

The same themes appear in Sutherland's book, *Constitutional Power and World Affairs*, published in 1919. He again distinguishes between internal and external powers.[122] When Great Britain entered into a peace treaty with America following the war for independence, "it is impossible to escape the conclusion that all powers of external sovereignty finally passed from the Kingdom of Great Britain to the people of the thirteen colonies as one political unit, and not to the people separately as thirteen political units."[123] In carrying out military operations, the President "must be given a free, as well as a strong hand. The contingencies of war are limitless — beyond the wit of man to foresee. . . . To rely on the slow and deliberate processes of legislation, after the situation and dangers and problems have arisen, may be to court danger — perhaps overwhelming disaster."[124] As will be explained in Section D, however, scholars have generally rejected his treatment of the Declaration of Independence, national sovereignty, and the sources and scope of presidential authority.

Regarding popular sovereignty, Sutherland was as inconsistent in his book as he was in his article. Early passages in the book state that "sovereignty — the plenary power to determine all questions of government without accountability to any one — is in the people and nowhere else."[125] The American Revolution "proceeded upon the principle that sovereignty belongs to the people, and it is by their consent, either express or implied, that the governing agency acts in any particular way, or acts at all. This is the animating principle of the Declaration of Independence. It is the very soul of the Constitution . . . ."[126] In an apparent rejection of inherent or extra-constitutional powers, Sutherland wrote this about the Constitution: "One of its great virtues is that it *fixes* the rules by which we are to govern . . . ."[127] He warned against "the danger of centralizing irrevocable and absolute power in the hands of a single ruler."[128] On "all matters of external sovereignty" and the general government, the "result does not flow from a claim of inherent power."[129]

Further into the book, however, Sutherland begins to flesh out the concepts of inherent and extra-constitutional powers as applied to external affairs and presidential authority. He described the Louisiana Purchase "as an exercise of the *inherent right of the United States as a Nation*."[130] What he attributed here to national power (exercised by both elected branches) he later attributed to independent presidential power. He acknowledged that the framers broke with Blackstone by placing many powers of external

---

[120] "Over *external* matters, however, no residuary powers do or can exist in the several States, and from the necessity of the case all necessary authority must be found in the National Government . . . ." *Id.* at 12 (emphasis in original).

[121] Id. at 8-9.

[122] George Sutherland, Constitutional Power and World Affairs 26 (1919).

[123] *Id.* at 38.

[124] *Id.* at 111.

[125] *Id.* at 2.

[126] *Id.* at 10.

[127] *Id.* at 13 (emphasis in original).

[128] *Id.* at 25.

[129] *Id.* at 47.

[130] *Id.* at 52 (emphasis in original).

affairs with Congress in Article I.[131] Yet once war is declared or waged, he saw in the President as Commander in Chief a power that is supreme: "Whatever any Commander-in-Chief may do under the laws and practices of war as recognized and followed by civilized nations, may be done by the President as Commander-in-Chief. In carrying on hostilities he possesses sole authority, and is charged with sole responsibility, and Congress is excluded from any direct interference."[132]

Martial law, when invoked, "finds no limitations in the Constitution, or in the general laws of the land."[133] Legislative or judicial checks do not exist: "The length of time during which military government shall be allowed to continue over conquered and acquired territory after the conclusion of a treaty of peace, is a matter wholly for political determination, in no manner controlled or affected by the Constitution, or subject to judicial review or determination."[134] Here Sutherland failed to take into account the judicial checks that have repeatedly placed limits on military occupation and martial law."[135]

In time of war, Sutherland argued that traditional rights and liberties had to be relinquished: "individual privilege and individual right, however dear or sacred, or however potent in normal times, must be surrendered by the citizen to strengthen the hand of the government lifted in the supreme gesture of war. Everything that he has, or is, or hopes to be — property, liberty, life — may be required."[136] Freedom of speech "may be curtailed or denied," along with freedom of the press.[137] Congress "has no power to directly interfere with, or curtail the war powers of the Commander-in-Chief."[138] Statutes enacted during World War I invested President Wilson "with virtual dictatorship over an exceedingly wide range of subjects and activities."[139] Sutherland spoke of the need to define the powers of external sovereignty as "unimpaired" and "unquestioned."[140]

C. Justice Sutherland

Writing for the Court in *Curtiss-Wright*, Justice Sutherland reversed the district court and upheld the delegation of legislative power to the President to place an embargo on arms or munitions to the Chaco. Whether or not the joint resolution "had related solely to internal affairs" it would be open to the challenge of unlawful delegation, which "we find it unnecessary to determine." The "whole aim of the resolution is to affect a situation entirely external to the United States, and falling within the category of foreign affairs."[141] Sutherland argued that the two categories of external and internal affairs are different

---

[131] *Id.* at 71.

[132] *Id.* at 75.

[133] *Id.* at 80.

[134] *Id.* at 82.

[135] *E.g.*, United States v. Brown, 12 U.S. (8 Cr.) 110, 128-29 (1814); Mitchell v. Harmony, 54 U.S. (13 How.) 115, 132-33, 135 (1851); Jecker v. Montgomery, 54 U.S. (13 How.) 498, 515 (1852); Untied States v. Anderson, 76 U.S. (9 Wall.) 56, 70-71 (1870); Dooley v. United States, 182 U.S. 222, 234, 235 (1901); *Ex parte* Orozco, 201 F. 106, 112 (W.D. Tex. 1912), *dismissed*, 229 U.S. 633 (1913).

[136] SUTHERLAND, CONSTITUTIONAL POWER AND WORLD AFFAIRS, at 98.

[137] *Id.*

[138] *Id.* at 109.

[139] *Id.* at 115.

[140] *Id.* at 171.

[141] United States v. Curtiss-Wright Corp., 299 U.S. 304, 315 (1936).

"both in respect of their origin and their nature."[142] The principle that the federal government is limited to either enumerated or implied powers "is categorically true only in respect of our internal affairs."[143] The purpose, he said, was "to carve from the general mass of legislative powers *then possessed by the states* such portions as it was thought desirable to vest in the federal government, leaving those not included in the enumeration still in the states."[144] But that doctrine, Sutherland insisted, "applies only to powers which the states had . . . since the states severally never possessed international powers . . . ."[145] The states may not have possessed "international" powers, but they did, as will be explained, possess and exercise sovereign powers.

To reach his conclusion, Sutherland said that after the Declaration of Independence "the powers of external sovereignty passed from the Crown not to the colonies severally, but to the colonies in their collective and corporate capacity as the United States of America."[146] By transferring external or foreign affairs directly to the national government, and then associating foreign affairs with the executive, Sutherland seemed to be in a position to argue for a broad definition of inherent presidential power.

There are two problems with his analysis. First, external sovereignty did not circumvent the colonies and the independent states and pass directly to the national government. When Great Britain entered into a peace treaty with America, the provisional articles of November 30, 1782 were not with a national government. Instead, "His Brittanic Majesty acknowledges the said United States, viz. New-Hampshire, Massachusetts-Bay, Rhode-Island and Providence Plantations, Connecticut, New-York, New-Jersey, Pennsylvania, Delaware, Maryland, Virginia, North-Carolina, South-Carolina, and Georgia," and referred to them as "free, sovereign and independent States."[147] The colonies formed a Continental Congress in 1774 and it provided a form of national government until passage of the Articles of Confederation, ratified in 1781, and the U.S. Constitution. Until that time, the states operated as sovereign entities in making treaties and exercising other powers that would pass to the new national government in 1789.

Second, sovereignty and external affairs did not pass from Great Britain to the U.S President. In 1776, at the time of America's break with England, there was no President and no separate executive branch. Only one branch of government, the Continental Congress, functioned at the national level. It carried out all governmental powers, including legislative, executive, and judicial.[148] When the new national government under the U.S. Constitution was established in 1789, sovereign powers were not placed solely in the President. They were divided between Congress and the President, with ultimate sovereignty vested in the people.

Much of *Curtiss-Wright* is devoted to Sutherland's discussion about independent and inherent presidential powers in foreign affairs. Having made the distinction between external and internal affairs, he wrote: "In this vast external realm, with its important, complicated, delicate and manifold problems, the President alone has the power to speak or listen as a representative of the nation. He *makes* treaties with the advice and consent of the Senate; but he alone negotiates. Into the field of negotiation the Senate

---

[142] *Id.*

[143] *Id.* at 316.

[144] *Id.* (emphasis in original).

[145] *Id.*

[146] *Id.*

[147] 8 Stat. 55 (1782).

[148] LOUIS FISHER, PRESIDENT AND CONGRESS 1-27, 253-70 (1972).

cannot intrude; and Congress itself is powerless to invade it."[149] In his book, Sutherland took a less rigid view. He recognized that Senators did in fact participate in the negotiation phase, and that Presidents often acceded to this "practical construction."[150] It was at this point of his decision that Sutherland quotes John Marshall out of context, implying a belief in presidential power that Marshall never embraced. Marshall said during House debate: "The President is the sole organ of the nation in its external relations, and its sole representative with foreign nations."[151] Justice Sutherland developed for the President a source of power in foreign affairs that was not grounded in authority delegated by Congress:

> It is important to bear in mind that we are here dealing not alone with an authority vested in the President by an exertion of legislative power, but with such an authority plus the very delicate, plenary and exclusive power of the President as the sole organ of the federal government in the field of international relations — a power which does not require as a basis for its exercise an act of Congress, but which, of course, like every other governmental power, must be exercised in subordination to the applicable provisions of the Constitution. It is quite apparent that if, in the maintenance of our international relations, embarrassment — perhaps serious embarrassment — is to be avoided and success for our aims achieved, congressional legislation which is to be made effective through negotiation and inquiry within the international field must often accord to the President a degree of discretion and freedom from statutory restriction which would not be admissible were domestic affairs alone involved.[152]

In freeing the President from statutory grants of power and legislative restrictions, Justice Sutherland did not explain how the exercise of presidential power would be constrained by requiring that it "be exercised in subordination to the applicable provisions of the Constitution." Which provisions in the Constitution could check or override presidential initiatives? On that he was silent. Justice McReynolds' dissent was brief: "He is of opinion that the court below reached the right conclusion and its judgment ought to be affirmed."[153]

Justice Stone did not participate. He later wrote to Edwin M. Borchard, a prominent law professor: "I have always regarded it as something of a misfortune that I was foreclosed from expressing my views in . . . *Curtiss-Wright* . . . because I was ill and away from the Court when it was decided."[154] In another letter to Borchard, Stone said he "should be glad to be disassociated" with Sutherland's opinion.[155] Borchard later advised Stone that the Court, in such cases as *Curtiss-Wright*, "has attributed to the Executive far more power than he had ever undertaken to claim."[156]

---

[149] 299 U.S. at 319 (emphasis in original).

[150] SUTHERLAND, CONSTITUTIONAL POWERS AND WORLD AFFAIRS, at 122-24. *See also* Louis Fisher, *Congressional Participation in the Treaty Process*, 137 U. PA. L. REV. 1511 (1989).

[151] 299 U.S. at 319.

[152] *Id.* at 319-20

[153] *Id.* at 333.

[154] Letter from Justice Harlan Fiske Stone to Edwin M. Borchard, Feb. 11, 1942; Papers of Harlan Fiske Stone, Container No. 6, Manuscript Room, Library of Congress.

[155] Letter from Stone to Borchard, May 13, 1937; Papers of Harlan Fiske Stone, Container No. 6, Manuscript Room, Library of Congress.

[156] Letter from Borchard to Stone, Feb. 9, 1942; Papers of Harlan Fiske Stone, Container No. 6, Manuscript Room, Library of Congress.

D. Evaluations by Scholars

A biography of Charles Evans Hughes, who served as Chief Justice on the *Curtiss-Wright* Court, states that Justice Sutherland "wrote a scholarly opinion confirming the broad sweep of the President's power in international affairs."[157] However, the biography provides no further details or analysis to justify the reference to scholarship. As expressed below, most of the studies of *Curtiss-Wright* in professional journals and books have been highly critical.

A student note in the *Georgetown Law Journal* in 1937 reviewed Sutherland's dicta concerning the President's "plenary and exclusive power," the sole-organ doctrine, and the availability of executive power independent of statutory authority.[158] The author was uncertain about the reach of the decision, but offered this assessment: "On the face of it the case is a long step toward executive autonomy in the field of foreign relations."[159] Similarly, another student note regarded the decision as recognizing "the President's superiority in conducting foreign affairs."[160]

A student note in the *Harvard Law Review* characterized the decision as "broad and novel" and not derived from the Constitution. It was, instead, rather "a heritage of the British Crown."[161] Another law review article, published in 1937, reiterated the main points of Sutherland's opinion without analyzing his assertions.[162] Writing for the *American Journal of International Law*, James W. Garner expressed general support for Sutherland's broad definition of presidential power in foreign affairs, but did not analyze such issues as the sole-organ doctrine, the transfer of sovereignty from England to the United States, or the availability of extra-constitutional powers.[163]

An article by Julius Goebel in 1938 attacked the principal tenets of Sutherland's opinion, concluding that his view of sovereignty "passing from the British crown to the union appears to be a perversion of the dictum of Jay, C. J. in *Chisholm's Executors v. Georgia,* 3 Dall. 419, 470 (U.S. 1799) to the effect that sovereignty passed from the crown to the people."[164] As to Sutherland's comment that the President "alone negotiates" treaties and that into this field the Senate "cannot intrude," Goebel regarded such views as "a somewhat misleading description of presidential authority in foreign affairs," citing earlier examples of Presidents consulting the Senate before negotiation.[165] To Goebel, Sutherland chose

---

[157] 2 MERLO J. PUSEY, CHARLES EVANS HUGHES 745 (1952).

[158] Constitutional Law — Delegation by Congress to President of Power in International Affairs, 25 GEO. L. J. 738, 739 (1937).

[159] *Id.* at 740.

[160] *Constitutional Law — Delegation of Legislative Power — Validity of Congressional Resolution and Presidential Proclamation Prohibiting Sale of Arms to Foreign Belligerents,* 6 BROOK. L. REV. 382, 383 (1937).

[161] *Constitutional Law — Separation of Powers — Delegation to President of Power to Declare Embargo,* 50 HARV. L. REV. 691, 692 (1937).

[162] Stefan A. Riesenfeld, *The Power of Congress and the President in International Relations: Three Recent Supreme Court Decisions,* 25 CAL. L. REV. 643, 665-69 (1937). For other generally descriptive student notes, *see Constitutional Law — Delegation of Powers — External Sovereignty,* 11 TEMP. L. Q. 418 (1937); *Constitutional Law — Delegation to President of Power to Declare Embargo on Exportation of Arms. United States v. Curtiss-Wright Export Corporation,* 1 MD. L. REV. 167 (1937); *Constitutional Law — Separation of Powers — Delegation to President of Power to Declare an Embargo,* 6 FORD. L. REV. 303 (1937).

[163] James W. Garner, *Executive Discretion in the Conduct of Foreign Relations,* 31 AM. J. INT'L L. 289 (1937).

[164] Julius Goebel, Jr., *Constitutional History and Constitutional Law,* 38 COLUM. L. REV. 555, 572 n.46 (1938).

[165] *Id.* n. 47.

"to frame an opinion in language closely parallel to the description of royal prerogative in foreign affairs in the *Ship Money Case*" of 1637.[166]

Writing in 1944, C. Perry Patterson regarded Sutherland's position on the existence of inherent presidential powers to be "(1) contrary to American history, (2) violative of our political theory, (3) unconstitutional, and (4) unnecessary, undemocratic, and dangerous."[167] He argued that the doctrine of *Curtiss-Wright* "that Congress acquired power over the entire field of foreign affairs as a result of the issue of the Declaration is contrary to the facts of American history."[168] Also writing in 1944, James Quarles objected to Sutherland's reasoning that foreign affairs, as distinguished from domestic affairs, invests the federal government with "powers which do not stem from the Constitution, are not granted, but are inherent."[169] He noted that the question of inherent presidential power was not "raised by counsel for either side, either in the District Court or in the Supreme Court; nor is there any allusion to any issue of that sort in the opinion of the District Judge. Indeed, the pages of Mr. Justice Sutherland's opinion devoted to a discussion of that question appear to the present writer as being little, if any, more than so much interesting yet discursive *obiter*."[170]

David M. Levitan, in 1946, not only found fault with Justice Sutherland's distinction between internal and external affairs and the belief that sovereignty flowed from the British crown directly to the national government, but expressed alarm about the implications for democratic government. Sutherland's theory marked "the furthest departure from the theory that [the] United States is a constitutionally limited democracy. It introduces the notion that national government possesses a secret reservoir of unaccountable power."[171] Levitan's review of the political and constitutional ideas at the time of the American Revolution and the Constitutional Convention left "little room for the acceptance of Mr. Justice Sutherland's 'inherent' powers, or, in fact, 'extra-constitutional' powers theory."[172] The Sutherland doctrine "makes shambles out of the very idea of a constitutionally limited government. It destroys even the symbol."[173]

Charles Lofgren and other scholars have pointed out that the states in 1776 operated as sovereign entities and not as part of a collective body, as Justice Sutherland claimed. The creation of a Continental Congress did not disturb the sovereign power of the states to make treaties, borrow money, solicit arms, lay embargoes, collect tariff duties, and conduct separate military campaigns.[174] The Supreme Court has recognized that the American colonies, upon their separation from England, exercised the powers of a

---

[166] *Id.* at 572-73. The Ship-Money Case is considered a landmark decision in defending the exercise of the royal prerogative to raise revenues against perceived dangers, notwithstanding statutory limitations. 3 St. Tr. 825, 1125-1243 (1816) [State Trials, edited by T. B. Howell].

[167] C. Perry Patterson, *In Re The United States v. The Curtiss-Wright Corporation*, 22 TEX. L. REV. 286, 297 (1944).

[168] *Id.* at 308.

[169] *James Quarles, The Federal Government: As to Foreign Affairs, Are Its Powers Inherent as Distinguished from Delegated?*, 32 GEO. L. J. 375, 376-77 (1944).

[170] *Id.* at 378.

[171] David M. Levitan, *The Foreign Relations Power: An Analysis of Mr. Justice Sutherland's Theory*, 55 YALE L. J. 467, 493 (1946).

[172] *Id.* at 496.

[173] *Id.* at 497.

[174] Charles Lofgren, *United States v. Curtiss-Wright Export Corporation: An Historical Reassessment*, 83 YALE L. J. 1 (1973); David M. Levitan, *The Foreign Relations Power: An Analysis of Mr. Justice Sutherland's Theory*, 55 YALE L. J. 467 (1946); Claude H. Van Tyne, *Sovereignty in the American Revolution: An Historical Study*, 12 AM. HIST. REV. 529 (1907).

sovereign and independent government.[175]   In 1796, the Court considered the Declaration of Independence to mean "not that the United Colonies *jointly*, in a *collective* capacity, were independent states, &c. but that *each* of them was a sovereign and independent state, that is, that *each* of them had a right to govern itself by its own authority, and its own laws, without any controul from any other power upon earth."[176]   To Lofgren, the historical evidence did not support Sutherland's reliance on inherent or extra-constitutional sources: "Federal power in foreign affairs rests on explicit and implicit constitutional grants and derives from the ordinary constitutive authority."[177]   Further: John Marshall in 1800 "evidently did not believe that because the President was the sole organ of communication and negotiation with other nations, he became the sole foreign policy-maker."[178]

Even if the power of sovereignty had somehow passed intact from the Crown to the national government, the U.S. Constitution allocates that power both to Congress and the President. The President and the Senate share the treaty power and the House of Representatives has discretion in deciding whether to appropriate funds needed to enforce treaties. The President receives ambassadors from other countries, but the Senate must approve U.S. ambassadors as part of the confirmation process. Congress has the power to declare war, issue letters of marque and reprisal, raise and support military forces, make rules for their regulation, provide for the calling up of the militia to suppress insurrections and repel invasions, and to provide for the organization and disciplining of the militia. The Constitution also explicitly grants to Congress the power to lay and collect duties on foreign trade, to regulate commerce with other nations, and to establish a uniform rule of naturalization.

Other studies have rejected the line of reasoning found in *Curtiss-Wright*. Michael Glennon described Sutherland's opinion as "a muddled law review article wedged with considerable difficulty between the pages of the United States Reports."[179]   Glennon asked how constitutional limits could possibly check Presidents who invoke inherent and extra-constitutional powers: "There is no logical reason why a power flowing from a source that transcends the Constitution should be subject to the prohibitions and limitations prescribed by the Constitution."[180]   Michael Ramsey offered a similar critique. The issue to Ramsey was not the broad scope of presidential power in foreign affairs, which he was prepared to concede. It was Sutherland's "claim that that power arose outside the Constitution."[181]

Roy Brownell wrote a more favorable assessment of *Curtiss-Wright*, concluding that Justice Sutherland had legitimate grounds for recognizing inherent presidential power in the field of national security and making the distinction he did between external and internal affairs.[182]   However, he also wrote that the "net result of *Curtiss-Wrights*'s deficiencies is that it places a disproportionate amount of

---

[175]   United States v. California, 332 U.S. 19, 31 (1947); Texas v. White, 74 U.S. 700, 725 (1869); M'Ilvaine v. Coxe's Lessee, 8 U.S. (4 Cr.) 209, 212 (1808); Ware v. Hylton, 3 U.S. (3 Dall.) 199, 222-24 (1796).

[176]   Ware v. Hylton, 3 U.S. (3 Dall.) at 224. *See also* Robins Island Preservation Fund v. Southold Dev., 755 F. Supp. 1185, 1189 (E.D.N.Y. 1991) (American states after the Declaration of Independence were sovereign and independent).

[177]   Lofgren, *United States v. Curtiss-Wright Export Corporation*, 83 YALE L. J. at 29-30.

[178]   *Id.* at 30.

[179]   Michael J. Glennon, *Two Views of Presidential Foreign Affairs Powe*r: Little v. Barreme or Curtiss-Wright?, 13 YALE J. INT'L L. 5, 13 (1988).

[180]   *Id.*

[181]   Michael D. Ramsey, *The Myth of Extraconstitutional Foreign Relations Power*, 42 WM. & MARY L. REV. 379, 382 (2000).

[182]   Roy E. Brownell II, *The Coexistence of* United States v. Curtiss-Wright *and* Youngstown Sheet & Tube v. Sawyer *in National Security Jurisprudence*, 16 J. L. & POL. 1, 21-39 (2000).

constitutional power in the hands of the Executive Branch vis-à-vis Congress. . . . The notion that Congress may be excluded from the conduct of national security affairs, as implied by *Curtiss-Wright*'s 'plenary/sole organ' passage, clearly does violence to the text of the Constitution."[183]

The dicta in Justice Sutherland's decision in *Curtiss-Wright* depend to a great degree on his ability to make a clear distinction between internal and external powers. Yet it is difficult, and often arbitrary, to draw a bright line between the two. In 1991, President George H. W. Bush remarked: "I guess my bottom line . . . is you can't separate foreign policy from domestic."[184] Two years later President Clinton expressed a similar view: "There is no longer a clear division between what is foreign and what is domestic."[185]

IX. Judicial Citations to "Sole Organ"

Anthony Simones, after reviewing the academic literature and judicial decisions following Sutherland's opinion, concluded that "for every scholar who hates *Curtiss-Wright*, there seems to exist a judge who loves it."[186] The litigation record supports that judgment. Courts repeatedly have cited *Curtiss-Wright* favorably, not only to sustain delegations of legislative power but also to support the existence of inherent and independent presidential power in foreign affairs.

Robert Jackson, as Attorney General, relied on *Curtiss-Wright* to defend the destroyers-bases agreement entered into by President Franklin D. Roosevelt in 1940.[187] Yet he also drew some boundaries to cabin executive power: "The President's power over foreign relations while 'delicate, plenary, and exclusive' is not unlimited. Some negotiations involve commitments as to the future which would carry an obligation to exercise powers vested in the Congress."[188] Two years later, in a case involving an executive agreement with Russia, the Supreme Court cited *Curtiss-Wright* and the "sole organ" doctrine, but described the President as acting under "a modest implied power"— not an inherent power.[189]

In the Nazi Saboteur Case of 1942, the Court spoke of the need to treat statutory grants of authority to the President as being "entitled to the greatest respect."[190] For that proposition it referred to three cases, including *Curtiss-Wright*.[191] At issue was authority granted by Congress, not inherent presidential power. In one of the Japanese-American cases, the Court looked to *Curtiss-Wright* to support the granting of broad powers to the President during wartime.[192] Again, the Court relied on Sutherland's opinion to sustain the delegation of legislative power, not the exercise of independent, exclusive and inherent executive powers.

---

[183] *Id.* at 40-41.

[184] PUBLIC PAPERS OF THE PRESIDENTS, 1991, II, at 1629.

[185] PUBLIC PAPERS OF THE PRESIDENTS, 1993, I, at 2.

[186] Anthony Simones, *The Reality* of Curtiss-Wright, 16 N. ILL. U. L. REV. 411, 415 (1996).

[187] 39 OPS. ATT'Y GEN. 484, 486-87 (1940).

[188] *Id.* at 487.

[189] United States v. Pink, 315 U.S. 203, 229 (1942). *Curtiss-Wright* was also cited in United States v. Belmont, 301 U.S. 324, 331-32 (1937).

[190] *Ex parte* Quirin, 317 U.S. 1, 41-42 (1942).

[191] *Id.* at 42.

[192] *Ex parte* Endo, 323 U.S. 283, 298 n.21 (1944).

In 1948, the Court decided that presidential actions in authorizing applications by carriers to engage in overseas air transportation were beyond the competence of the courts to adjudicate.[193] The President was acting under a provision of the Civil Aeronautics Act. The Court's opinion, written by Justice Jackson, cited *Curtiss-Wright* and adopted much of its language, but the thrust of the decision was to remove the judiciary, not Congress, from these questions:

> The President, both as Commander-in-Chief and as the Nation's organ for foreign affairs, has available intelligence services whose reports are not and ought not to be published in the world. It would be intolerable that courts, without the relevant information, should review and perhaps nullify actions of the Executive taken on information properly held secret. Nor can courts sit *in camera* in order to be taken into executive confidences. But even if courts could require full disclosure, the very nature of executive decisions as to foreign policy is political, not judicial. Such decisions are wholly confided by our Constitution to the political departments of the government, Executive and Legislative. They are delicate, complex, and involve large elements of prophecy. They are and should be undertaken only by those directly responsible to the people whose welfare they advance or imperil. They are decisions of a kind for which the Judiciary has neither aptitude, facilities nor responsibility and which has long been held to belong in the domain of political power not subject to judicial intrusion or inquiry. *Coleman* v. *Miller*, 307 U.S. 433, 454; *United States* v. *Curtiss-Wright Corp.*, 299 U.S. 304, 319-321; *Oetjen* v. *Central Leather Co.*, 246 U.S. 297, 302.[194]

When Justice Jackson wrote those words, courts had in fact been hearing executive confidences *in camera* as part of a judge's duty to determine what evidence could be admitted at trial.[195] Moreover, in recent years, Congress has specifically authorized federal courts to receive confidential documents from the executive branch and examine them in camera.[196]

In a military tribunal case decided in 1948, Justice William O. Douglas said in a concurrence: "The President is the sole organ of the United States in the field of foreign relations. See *United States* v. *Curtiss-Wright Corp.*, 299 U.S. 304, 318-321. Agreements which he has made with our Allies in furtherance of our war efforts have been legion. Whether they are wise or unwise, necessary or improvident, are political questions, not justiciable ones."[197] As with Justice Jackson above, this passage appears to exclude the judiciary, not Congress, and does not seem to endorse unlimited, unchecked presidential actions taken pursuant to inherent powers.

In 1950, the Court used *Curtiss-Wright* to support an inherent presidential power to exclude aliens. The case involved questions of statutory authority and agency regulations adopted to enforce the statute, but the Court also relied on inherent presidential power: "there is no question of inappropriate delegation of legislative power involved here. The exclusion of aliens is a fundamental act of sovereignty. The right to do so stems not alone from legislative power but is inherent in the executive power to control the foreign affairs of the nation. *United States* v. *Curtiss-Wright Export Corp.*, 299 U.S.

---

[193] C.&S. Air Lines v. Waterman Corp., 333 U.S. 103 (1948).

[194] *Id.* at 111.

[195] Haugen v. United States, 253 F.2d 850, 851 (9th Cir. 1946).

[196] *E.g.,* 88 Stat. 1562 (1974) (a district court has jurisdiction "to enjoin the agency from withholding agency records and to order the production of any agency records improperly withheld from the complainant. In such a case the court . . . may examine the contents of such agency records in camera . . ."). *See* Ronald M. Levin, *In Camera Inspections Under the Freedom of Information Act*, 41 U. CHI. L. REV. 557 (1974). The Classified Information Act of 1980 authorizes trial judges to rule on classified information in camera before the defendant attempts to introduce evidence in open court. 94 Stat. 2025 (1980).

[197] Hirota v. MacArthur, 338 U.S. 197, 208 (1948). The concurrence by Justice Douglas was announced June 27, 1949.

304; *Fong Yue Ting* v. *United States*, 149 U.S. 698, 713. When Congress prescribes a procedure concerning the admissibility of aliens, it is not dealing alone with a legislative power. It is implementing an inherent executive power."[198]

This ruling would support the exercise of inherent executive power taken in the absence of congressional policy. It is less clear how a court would rule if presidential action violated statutory policy. In another military tribunal case, decided in 1950, the Court discussed legal challenges being brought against the "conduct of diplomatic and foreign affairs, for which the President is exclusively responsible. *United States* v. *Curtiss-Wright Corp.*, 299 U.S. 304; . . . ."[199] A deportation case in 1952 cited *Curtiss-Wright* but nevertheless recognized the role of the legislative branch in deciding policy in this area. Aliens "remain subject to the plenary power of Congress to expel them under the sovereign right to determine what noncitizens shall be permitted to remain within our borders."[200]

In the Steel Seizure Case of 1952, Justice Jackson observed that the most that can be drawn from *Curtiss-Wright* is the intimation that the President "might act in external affairs without congressional authority, but not that he might act contrary to an act of Congress."[201] He noted that "much of the [Justice Sutherland] opinion is *dictum*."[202] In 1981, a federal appellate court cautioned against placing undue reliance on "certain dicta" in Justice Sutherland's opinion: "To the extent that denominating the President as the 'sole organ' of the United States in international affairs constitutes a blanket endorsement of plenary Presidential power over any matter extending beyond the borders of this country, we reject that characterization."[203]

A right to travel case in 1965 cited *Curtiss-Wright* in upholding the authority of the Secretary of State to restrict travel to Cuba.[204] Inherent presidential power, however, was not at issue. The case turned on the Court's recognition that Congress, in delegating legislative power to the President, "must of necessity paint with a brush broader than that it customarily wields in domestic areas."[205] Several Justices in the Pentagon Papers Case in 1971 made reference to *Curtiss-Wright*. In a concurrence, joined by Justice Byron White, Justice Potter Stewart described the President's power in national defense and international affairs as "largely unchecked by the Legislative and Judicial branches."[206] He left unclear whether the lack of checks was constitutionally mandated or merely a reflection of Congress and the courts not doing their jobs. The reference to Justice Sutherland's decision is included in a footnote related to the judicial branch, suggesting that *Curtiss-Wright* stands as a limiting factor on the judiciary, not on Congress. A concurrence by Justice Thurgood Marshall recognized that *Curtiss-Wright* gives the President "broad powers by virtue of his primary responsibility for the conduct of our foreign affairs and his position as Commander in Chief."[207] A dissent by Justice John Harlan quoted John Marshall's speech in 1800 ("The President is the sole organ of the nation in its external relations, and its sole representation

---

[198] Knauff . Shaughnessy, 338 U.S. 537, 542 (1950).

[199] Johnson v. Eisentrager, 339 U.S. 763, 789 (1950).

[200] Carlson v. Landon, 342 U.S. 524, 534 (1952).

[201] Youngstown Co. v. Sawyer, 343 U.S. 579, 636 n.2 (1952) (concurring opinion).

[202] *Id.*

[203] American Intern. Group v. Islamic Republic of Iran, 657 F.2d 430, 438 n.6 (D.C. Cir. 1981).

[204] Zemel v. Rusk, 381 U.S. 1, 17 (1965).

[205] *Id.*

[206] New York Times Co. v. United States, 403 U.S. 713, 727 (1971).

[207] *Id.* at 741.

with foreign nations") and remarked: "From that time, shortly after the founding of the Nation, to this, there has been no substantial challenge to this description of the scope of executive power."[208] A citation to *Curtiss-Wright* is added at that point. The problem with "this description of the scope of executive power" is that Marshall's sentence, standing by itself, does not delineate any particular scope of presidential power, and the context of the House debate refutes any notion that Marshall believed in exclusive, inherent, or unchecked executive power. What is meant by "this description of the scope of executive power" — what Marshall meant or how Sutherland misconceived what Marshall said?

A year after the Pentagon Papers Case, Justice William H. Rehnquist announced the judgment of the Court in a case involving the expropriation of property in Cuba. He first cited a case from 1918 that recognized that the "conduct of the foreign relations of our Government is committed by the Constitution to the Executive and Legislative — 'the political' — Departments . . . ."[209] Having discussed *concurrent* power, he then proceeded down the opposite path by citing *Curtiss-Wright* and quoting from Marshall's sole-organ speech to buttress the point that the executive branch has "exclusive competence" in the field of foreign affairs.[210] In other decisions, Rehnquist also used *Curtiss-Wright* to argue that the limits on the authority of Congress to delegate its legislative power are "less stringent in cases where the entity exercising the delegated authority itself possesses independent authority over the subject matter,"[211] and that the President occupies a "pre-eminent position . . . with respect to our Republic," particularly "in the area of foreign affairs and international relations."[212]

In a treaty termination case decided in 1979, Justice Lewis Powell relied on *Curtiss-Wright* to argue that Congress may grant the President wider discretion in foreign policy than in domestic affairs,[213] whereas in the same case Justice Rehnquist (joined by Chief Justice Warren Burger and Justices Stewart and John Paul Stevens) cited *Curtiss-Wright* for the more sweeping proposition that the judiciary should decline to decide political questions involving "foreign relations — specifically a treaty commitment to use military force in the defense of a foreign government if attacked."[214] A year later, in a concurrence, Rehnquist cited *Curtiss-Wright* to observe that delegations of legislative authority are upheld "because of the delegatee's residual authority over particular subjects of regulation," and that in the area of foreign affairs Congress (quoting from Justice Sutherland) "must often accord to the President a degree of discretion and freedom from statutory restriction which would not be admissible were domestic affairs alone involved."[215]

In 1981, in a case involving the revocation of an American citizen's passport, Chief Justice Burger relied in part on language from *Curtiss-Wright* that the President "has his confidential sources of information. He has his agents in the form of diplomatic, consular and other officials. Secrecy in respect of information gathered by them may be highly necessary, and the premature disclosure of it productive of harmful results."[216] In the same year, Justice Rehnquist wrote for the Court in sustaining President

---

[208] Id. at 756.

[209] First Nat. City Bk. v. Banco Nacional de Cuba, 406 U.S. 759, 766 (1972) (citing Oetjen v. Central Leather Co., 246 U.S. 297, 302 (1918)).

[210] *Id.* (citing United States v. Belmont, 301 U.S. 324 (1937)).

[211] United States v. Mazurie, 419 U.S. 544, 556-57 (1975).

[212] Nixon v. Administrator of General Services, 433 U.S. 425, 550-51 n.6 (1977) (dissenting op.).

[213] Goldwater v. Carter, 444 U.S. 996, 1001 n.1 (1980).

[214] *Id.* at 1003-04. *See also* 1004-05.

[215] Industrial Union Dept. v. American Petrol. Inst., 448 U.S. 607, 684 (1980).

[216] Haig v. Agee, 453 U.S. 280, 307-08 (1981).

Jimmy Carter's decision to freeze Iranian assets. The decision turned in large part on statutory authority under the International Emergency Economic Powers Act (IEEPA), but Rehnquist referred to language in *Curtiss-Wright* about the existence of presidential power "which does not require as a basis for its exercise an act of Congress."[217] The Court took note of the fact that "Congress has not disapproved of the action taken here. . . . We are thus clearly not confronted with a situation in which Congress has in some way resisted the exercise of Presidential authority."[218] This seems to imply a legislative check on presidential power that does not "require as a basis for its exercise an act of Congress."

In 1984, the Court upheld presidential authority under the Trading With the Enemy Act (TWEA) to limit travel-related transactions with Cuba, referring to language in *Curtiss-Wright* about the "traditional deference to executive judgment '[i]n this vast external realm.'"[219] A 1988 decision by the Supreme Court concerned the authority of the Central Intelligence Agency (CIA) to terminate an employee on grounds of homosexuality. The Court decided that a provision of the Administrative Procedure Act precluded judicial review of the agency's decision, and reversed the D.C. Circuit on that ground.[220] Concurring in part and dissenting in part, Justice Sandra Day O'Connor stated that the functions performed by the CIA "lie at the core of 'the very delicate, plenary and exclusive power of the President as the sole organ of the federal government in the field of international relations.' *United States* v. *Curtiss-Wright Export Corp.*, 299 U.S. 304, 320 (1936)."[221] In a dissent, Justice Antonin Scalia repeated the same language, adding the rest of the sentence from *Curtiss-Wright*: "a power which does not require as a basis for its exercise an act of Congress."[222]

In 1993, the Supreme Court held that neither a statutory provision nor Article 33 of the United Nations Convention Relating to the Status of Refugees limited the President's power to order the Coast Guard to return undocumented aliens, intercepted on the high seas, to Haiti.[223] The Court interpreted congressional legislation as granting to the President "ample power to establish a naval blockade that would simply deny illegal Haitian migrants the ability to disembark on our shores."[224] Whether the President's method of returning Haitians posed a greater risk of harm to them was considered "irrelevant to the scope of his authority to take action that neither the Convention nor the statute clearly prohibits."[225] The presumption that a congressional statute does not have extraterritorial application unless the intent is clear "has special force when we are construing treaty and statutory provisions that may involve foreign and military affairs for which the President has unique responsibility. Cf. *United States* v. *Curtiss-Wright Export Corp.*, 299 U.S. 304 (1936)."[226] Left unexplored in the 1993 decision was the constitutional authority of Congress to legislate and reshape national policy in this area.

---

[217] Dames & Moore v. Regan, 453 U.S. 654, 661 (1981).

[218] *Id.* at 687-88.

[219] Regan v. Wald, 468 U.S. 222, 243 (1984).

[220] Webster v. Doe, 486 U.S. 592 (1988).

[221] *Id.* at 605-06.

[222] *Id.* at 614-15.

[223] Sale v. Haitian Centers Council, Inc., 509 U.S. 155 (1993).

[224] *Id.* at 187.

[225] *Id.* at 188.

[226] *Id.*

X. Conclusions

Curtiss-Wright remains a frequent citation used by the judiciary to uphold broad definitions of presidential power in foreign relations. Scholarly criticism has been directed at these points: the reliance on dicta in Justice Sutherland's opinion, taking John Marshall's speech out of context, and arguing that sovereignty passed directly from England to the national government and particularly to the President. Also objected to is Sutherland's distinction between external and internal affairs for the purpose of vesting exclusive powers with the President. The case is frequently cited by the courts to support not only broad delegations of legislative power to the executive branch, but also the existence of independent, implied, inherent, and extra-constitutional powers for the President.[227] Although some Justices of the Supreme Court have described the President's foreign relations power as "exclusive," the Court itself has not denied to Congress its constitutional authority to enter the field and reverse or modify presidential decisions in the area of national security and foreign affairs.

In *Hamdan* v. *Rumsfeld*, decided by the Court on June 29, 2006, the Bush administration had argued that the inherent powers available to the President under Article II included authority to create military commissions and to adopt necessary trial procedures. Presidential power under Article II "includes the inherent authority to create military commissions even in the absence of any statutory authorization, because that authority is a necessary and longstanding component of his war powers."[228] According to the government, "[t]hroughout our Nation's history, Presidents have exercised their inherent commander-in-chief authority to establish military commissions without any specific authorization from Congress."[229] The government cited *Curtiss-Wright* for the proposition that the President may determine that the Geneva Convention does not apply to al Qaeda in Afghanistan or elsewhere, and that al Qaeda detainees do not qualify as prisoners of war.[230]

In *Hamdan*, the Court held that the military commission created by the administration was not expressly authorized by any congressional statute. Existing law, including Article 21, did not provide a mandate to the President to authorize any type of commission he deemed necessary, nor did the Court find anything in the text or legislative history of the Authorization for Use of Military Force (AUMF), enacted after 9/11, that intended to expand or alter the authorization set forth in Article 21. The Court found that the military commission established by the administration, in terms of structure and procedures, violated both the Uniform Code of Military Justice (UCMJ) and the four Geneva Conventions. It also found that UCMJ Article 36 had not been complied with and that the rules adopted for Hamdan's commission were illegal. As a result, it was necessary for the administration to come to Congress to obtain statutory authority to proceed in a legal manner. In so ruling, the Court did not accept the government's position that the President has inherent authority under the Commander in Chief Clause or other Article II powers to create military commissions without first obtaining authority from Congress.

---

[227] Justice Sutherland was not the first, in *Curtiss-Wright*, to recognize inherent powers for the President. *See*, for example, Kennett v. Chambers, 55 U.S. 38, 51 (1852) (President's power to recognize other governments), and *In re* Neagle, 135 U.S. 1, 64 (1890) (where the Court refers not only to express powers but also to "the rights, duties and obligations growing out of the Constitution itself, our international relations, and all the protection implied by the nature of the government under the Constitution").

[228] Brief for Respondents, Hamdan v. Rumsfeld, No. 05-184, Supreme Court of the United States, February 2006, at 21.

[229] *Id.* at 22.

[230] *Id.* at 38.

Curtiss-Wright is not mentioned in the decision for the Court by Justice Stevens, the concurrences by Justices Breyer and Kennedy, or the dissents by Justices Scalia and Alito. The decision is cited twice in the dissent by Justice Thomas (pages 43 and 48 of his memo op.).

About the Author

Louis Fisher is a specialist in constitutional law with the Law Library of the Library of Congress, after working for the Congressional Research Service from 1970 to March 6, 2006. During his service with CRS he was research director of the House Iran-Contra Committee in 1987, writing major sections of the final report. Fisher received his doctorate in political science from the New School for Social Research and has taught at a number of universities and law schools.

His books include *President and Congress* (1972), *Presidential Spending Power* (1975), *The Constitution Between Friends* (1978), *The Politics of Shared Power* (4th ed. 1998), *Constitutional Conflicts Between Congress and the President* (4th ed. 1997), *Constitutional Dialogues* (1988), *American Constitutional Law* (6th ed. 2005), *Presidential War Power* (2d ed. 2004), *Political Dynamics of Constitutional Law* (with Neal Devins, 4th ed. 2006), *Congressional Abdication on War and Spending* (2000), *Religious Liberty in America* (2002), *Nazi Saboteurs on Trial* (2003; 2d ed. 2005), *The Politics of Executive Privilege* (2004), *The Democratic Constitution* (with Neal Devins, 2004), *Military Tribunals and Presidential Power* (2005), and *In the Name of National Security* (2006). With Leonard W. Levy, he edited the four-volume *Encyclopedia of the American Presidency* (1994), which was awarded the Dartmouth Medal. He has twice won the Louis Brownlow Book Award and in 2006 he received the Neustadt Book Award for *Military Tribunals and Presidential Power*.

Dr. Fisher has been invited to testify before Congress on such issues as war powers, CIA whistleblowing, covert spending executive privilege, executive spending discretion, presidential reorganization authority, Congress and the Constitution, the legislative veto, the item veto, the pocket veto, recess appointments, the budget process, the Gramm-Rudman-Hollings Act, the balanced budget amendment, biennial budgeting, presidential impoundment powers, and executive lobbying,

He has been active with CEELI (Central and East European Law Initiative) of the American Bar Association, the International Bar Association, and the Library of Congress in helping other countries draft new constitutions. Fisher filed four amicus briefs in military tribunal cases (Padilla and Hamdan) and recently filed an amicus brief in a case brought by the Center for Constitutional Rights regarding NSA eavesdropping. He has been invited to speak in Albania, Australia, Belgium, Bulgaria, Canada, China, the Czech Republic, England, France, Germany, Greece, Israel, Japan, Macedonia, Malaysia, Mexico, the Netherlands, Oman, the Philippines, Poland, Romania, Russia, Slovenia, South Korea, Taiwan, Ukraine, and the United Arab Emirates.